HOW TO KNIT

Learn the Basic Stitches and Techniques

Leslie Ann Bestor

Storey Publishing

*The mission of Storey Publishing is to serve our customers by
publishing practical information that encourages
personal independence in harmony with the environment.*

Edited by Gwen Steege and Kathy Brock
Series design by Alethea Morrison
Art direction by Cynthia N. McFarland and Jeff Stiefel
Text production by Theresa Wiscovitch
Indexed by Eileen Clawson

Cover illustration by © Caitlin Keegan
Interior illustrations by Gayle Isabelle Ford

Storey Publishing
210 MASS MoCA Way
North Adams, MA 01247
www.storey.com

Printed in the United States by McNaughton & Gunn, Inc.
10 9 8 7 6 5 4 3 2 1

LIBRARY OF CONGRESS CATALOGING-IN-PUBLICATION DATA

Bestor, Leslie Ann, author.
  How to knit / by Leslie Ann Bestor.
      pages cm — (Storey basics)
  Includes bibliographical references and index.   5580   8512   10/14
  ISBN 978-1-61212-359-2 (pbk. : alk. paper)
  ISBN 978-1-61212-360-8 (ebook) 1. Knitting. I. Title.
TT820.B5985 2014
746.43'2—dc23
                              2014020871

CONTENTS

AN INVITATION TO KNIT

The daughter of a reference librarian and a professor, I grew up with a love of books and learning. As an adult, when I decided to take my meager, self-taught knitting skills to a new level and become a "professional" knitter, my mother, though horrified at the prospect of my ruined résumé, promptly went down to her local yarn store and asked the owner to recommend books.

She sent me a stack, and I pretended I was in fiber college and studied and practiced and knit. Fast-forward 30 years, and I am now working in that same yarn store, spending my days as a "yarn therapist," counseling both new and experienced knitters on techniques, patterns, and yarns. I am a teacher at heart and take great satisfaction in seeing people get it.

A lot of people come into the yarn store and ask for books for beginning knitters. There are many fine ones out there, but the few that I really like and recommend are the ones that make me feel like I'm chatting with a friend. Such books are casual, inviting, and full of useful information that is easy to understand. When my editor first asked me to write this book, I had to really think about why we needed another learn-to-knit book. If you're a new knitter, here's what I hope this book will provide.

Accessibility. I want this book to make readers feel welcomed, like you're sitting down with a good friend who is also an expert teacher. I want to provide both encouragement and humor.

Simplicity. When learning something new, it's easy to get overwhelmed by the details, and many books try to include everything one would ever need to know about knitting. It's like being handed a college textbook when you really just want a few basic instructions to see if you even like knitting. However, writing a useful beginner's book is not a matter of dumbing things down; rather, it involves stripping down the information to the basic techniques. That is what I try to do in this book, because I know you can start knitting right now with a few simple instructions, even if you don't yet know the intricacies of yarn plies and sheep breeds.

So I invite you to sit with me and learn to knit. This book will give you the basics, toss in a little more useful information at the end, and start you down this lovely path. Follow it where you will, and enjoy the journey.

If you're like me, you just want to get going, hop right in, and get the yarn on the needles. That's why this book is arranged a little differently from many learn-to-knit books, and my suggestions may sound a bit radical. The great part is that this is only a book, there are no knitting police, and you can jump around as you want. And I encourage you to do so! The truth is, we all learn in different ways, and with something as kinesthetic as knitting, it will help if you let go and experiment with various ways to hold your hands and hold the yarn until you find what works for you.

The other thing I strongly suggest is to let go of the expectation many adults have that they will master a new skill effortlessly and perfectly the first time. Take your cues from children, who do not expect to get it right the first time, but keep trying until they do. Knitting can be blissful and relaxing, meditative and creative. But the first time you try to manipulate two sticks and an unruly piece of string — probably not so much.

The important thing is to persevere and think of all the beautiful creations you want to make. You will get there, and it will be glorious. The first items off your needles will probably not be the perfect gift for anyone except your mother, but before long, you will be proud to gift your handknits to the world at large (not to mention adorning your body with their splendor).

SHORTCUT TO GETTING STARTED

I CONSIDER MYSELF LUCKY if you have read this far, rather than jumping right to the first instructions, and I will try to cut to the chase. There are chapters about needles and fibers (mind you, they are full of really good information that you will appreciate and refer back to one day), but I put them at the back, knowing you just want to get going *now*. The important information from those chapters covers the supplies you need to start knitting:

- A ball of good-quality worsted-weight wool in a light color (until you are comfortable with your knitting, no multicolors, lumpy-bumpies, or fuzzy yarn)
- A pair of 9" or 10" wood or bamboo straight needles in U.S. size 8 or 9 (5 or 5.5 mm)

The next step may sound a little crazy — get someone to cast on for you and jump straight to the knitting part! Seriously! Casting on requires more coordination than just knitting, and getting stuck there can lead many to abandon knitting before they even get to the first stitch. So if you've got a friend who knits, have him or her cast on 20 stitches and knit the first row, then hand the needles to you so that you can jump right into chapter 2 with the knit and purl stitches. After you're comfortable wrangling needles and yarn, go back to learn one of the cast ons to begin your next piece. If you have no such ally, start with one of the cast ons in chapter 1 and then move on to chapter 2 to begin your stitching adventures. Off we go, and good luck!

A Note for Left-Handers

Knitting is a two-handed skill, and neither hand dominates the proceedings. Because of that, the basic way to knit works well for either left- or right-handed knitters. Although it is possible to knit "left-handed" by mirroring the motions of right-handed knitters, doing so usually creates problems, because many techniques do not translate as mirror images. In knitting, both hands work together; it is not like being forced to use right-handed scissors. And trust me on this: knitting feels awkward for all beginners, regardless of their handedness.

CHAPTER 1

WHEN YOU'RE READY TO CAST ON

To begin to knit, you need to first put stitches on your needles. This is called *casting on,* and there are dozens of ways to do it, some that are specific to certain situations, such as making socks or lace items, and some that are more general. I am going to show you a couple of all-purpose cast ons that will serve you well through your initial forays into knitting. As you progress, you may want to learn others, and I humbly suggest my book *Cast On, Bind Off* to further your education.

SLIP KNOT

The slip knot creates a loop that can be placed on a needle to begin your cast on. You make it like this:

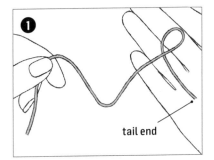

tail end

1. Make a loop of your yarn with the tail end underneath the long end where the yarns overlap.

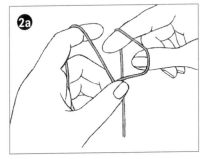

2. Reach through the loop (a), grab the long yarn, and pull a new loop through the first loop (b). Place this loop on your needle and pull both ends to tighten.

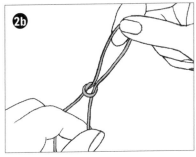

KNITTED CAST ON

This cast on is easy to remember because it is a lot like a regular knit stitch, making it a common cast on for beginners. The edge is fairly firm, though it may stretch out of shape, and it looks good from both sides. This cast on can also be worked in the middle or at the end of a row, when you need to add extra stitches to a work in progress.

1. Make a slip knot, leaving a 6-inch tail, and place it on the needle.

2. Hold the needle with the slip knot in your left hand and an empty needle in your right hand.

3. Insert the tip of the right-hand needle into the left side of the slip knot, going from front to back. Using the strand of yarn attached to the ball, wrap the yarn around the right needle tip, coming first underneath the needle and then over the top to the back. Pull the right tip forward, catching the wrapped yarn, and draw it through the loop on the left needle without letting either stitch drop off the needles.

ball yarn

yarn tail

4. Transfer the new stitch on your right needle to the left needle by twisting the right needle so the two needles are side by side; then insert the left tip into the bottom of the new stitch

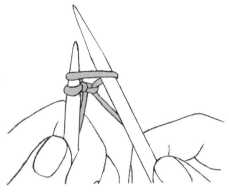

and slide the right needle out. Be careful to slide the new stitch all the way onto the thick part of the needle before tightening it. If you tighten while it is still on the tip, the new stitch will be too tight, and you will likely curse loudly when you have to work with it on the next row.

Continue in this manner, knitting into the endmost stitch on the left needle and transferring the new stitch back to the left needle until you have the desired number of stitches.

Getting a Hold on the Needles

Hold the needles comfortably, near the tips. It's kind of like holding a toothbrush — your lower fingers grasp the lower half of the needle in the palm of your hand, and your index finger and thumb are near the tip, to control the movements.

LONG-TAIL CAST ON

This is the workhorse of the cast ons, and many people use it for everything. And, frankly, if you learn only one cast on, this is the one to know because of its great versatility. That said, learning the long-tail cast on can be a bit tricky because in addition to juggling the needle and the yarn, you need to maintain that darn slingshot position — which I describe below. (So, as I suggested in the introduction, you may want to get a friend to cast on the first time for you.) I know, I know, sometimes you just have to dive into the deep end, so here we go.

SLINGSHOT POSITION

Setup 1. Measure out a long tail. To measure the amount needed to cast on 10 stitches, wrap your yarn around the needle 10 times, pull it off, and measure it. That is how much you need for 10 stitches with that particular yarn-and-needle combo. If you want to cast on 20 stitches, double this length; for 30 stitches, triple it, and so on. Then add a few extra inches.

Setup 2. Make a slip knot at the point you measured, and put the slip knot on the needle. (You need only one needle for this cast on.) Hold the needle in your right hand and let the two yarn ends dangle down, with the tail end closest to your body.

Setup 3. Pinch the tips of your left forefinger and thumb together and poke them between the strands of yarn. With the other three fingers of your left hand, grasp the yarn in the palm of your hand. Spread your thumb and forefinger apart, and rotate them back and up so they are pointing to the sky. Looks like a slingshot, right? Okay, now you're ready to cast on, long-tail style.

SETUP FOR LONG-TAIL CAST ON

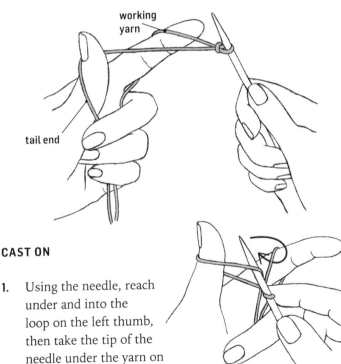

working yarn

tail end

CAST ON

1. Using the needle, reach under and into the loop on the left thumb, then take the tip of the needle under the yarn on your left forefinger from right to left.

2. Pull up a loop and bring it through the thumb loop.

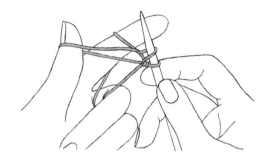

3. Drop the yarn off your left thumb and gently tighten (not too tight!) the loop on the needle.

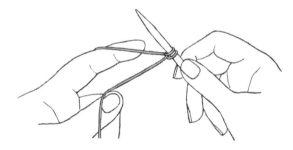

Repeat these steps for the desired number of stitches. See, it's really not that hard, just a bit awkward at first.

Note: Because of how the long-tail cast on forms the stitches, it essentially knits the first row for you. That means the first row you work will be a wrong-side row.

CHAPTER 2

THE BASIC STITCHES:
KNIT, PURL, AND . . . SLIP

Ready? It's time to begin knitting! In knitting, there are only two stitches that are the building blocks for an infinite variety of stitch patterns, all of which are just a maneuvering of these two humble stitches. I suggest that you approach your new craft by getting comfortable with them.

- **Knit stitch.** Cast on 20 stitches and learn the knit stitch. Practice the stitch for many rows until it feels sort of comfortable and you end up with the same number of stitches on every row. This will give you a garter-stitch swatch (see page 29).
- **Purl stitch.** With those stitches still on the needles, learn to purl, and practice that for a bunch of rows. Look — more garter!

Then learn how to end: bind off the stitches (see It's Over: Binding Off, page 32). Ta-da! You made a thing! You can fold it up and sew around the edges. Voilà — a pot holder! Or a coaster! Or a pouch! Be proud, you are a knitter!

At the beginning of a row, regardless of whether it is right side or wrong side, knit or purl, the needle in your left hand will have the stitches ready to be worked. Your right-hand needle will be empty. Hold the needles comfortably, near the tips. The yarn dangles from the stitch at the tip of the needle, and you pick up the yarn and tension it in your left hand for Continental knitting or in the right hand for English style. (See Continental versus English on the facing page.)

A Note on Semantics

The word knit *can be somewhat confusing as it describes the act of knitting, which includes both knit and purl stitches, as well as the knit stitch itself. To keep things clear, I will use the term* work, *as in "work to the end of the row." A stitch that is worked can be either a knit stitch or a purl stitch.*

Continental versus English

There are as many ways to hold the needles and wrap the yarn as there are grandmothers who have passed knitting techniques on to their grandchildren. The two main styles are called Continental and English, and the basic difference between the two is about which hand holds the yarn.

- **In Continental knitting**, the yarn is held in the left hand, and the knitter uses the right-hand needle to scoop or grab the yarn and pull it through the stitch.
- **In English Knitting**, the yarn is held in the right hand and wrapped around the right needle tip before the stitch is pulled through.

As with any technique, there are advocates of both styles, some more vocal and convinced of the rightness of their choice than others. I am of the school of doing what feels right in your hands. If you already know how to crochet, you may find Continental easier, because the yarn is held the same as in crochet. If you are starting from scratch, pick a style and stick with it for a while to see how it works. Since you are just beginning, at first nothing may feel right or comfortable. Give yourself a chance to gain some competence in one style before trying another, to avoid confusing yourself.

KNIT STITCH KNOW-HOW

ENGLISH STYLE

Setup. Position the yarn so it runs from the end stitch on the left needle, over your right index finger, and through your right hand to the ball of yarn. You will need to maintain some tension on the yarn to be able to knit. Refer to the illustrations below and on the next page for two ways to wrap and tension the yarn. And know, too, that there are many more ways besides these examples. You will have to experiment to find what works best for you.

TENSION METHOD 1: Wrap the yarn in and out between your fingers and use your lower fingers to grasp it. Keep the yarn close to the first knuckle on your index finger.

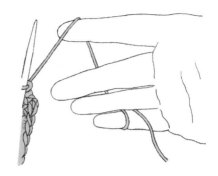

TENSION METHOD 2:
Wrap the yarn over your index finger and wrap it around your pinkie finger.

1. Holding the yarn in back of the needles, insert the tip of the right needle through the stitch on the tip of the left needle from left to right so the right needle pokes through to the back; the right needle should be underneath the left needle.

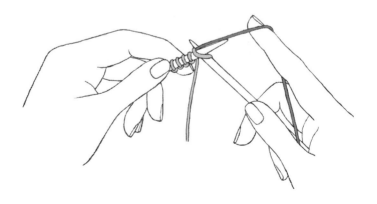

2. Wrap the yarn around the right needle tip, coming from underneath, then over the top and to the right.

3. Holding the wrapped yarn firmly, pull the right needle forward through the stitch (a), letting the old stitch fall off the tip of the left needle (b). You've made a knit stitch!

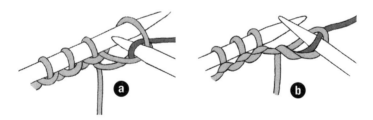

Repeat these steps across the row until all stitches have been knit off the left needle. Then move the needle full of stitches to your left hand and the empty needle to your right hand, and knit back across the row. It may feel awkward at first, but give it some time.

CONTINENTAL STYLE

Setup. Position the yarn so it goes from the end stitch, over your left index finger, and through your left hand to the ball of yarn. As with English style, there are many ways to keep tension on the yarn. Some folks wrap or pinch the yarn between their lower fingers (a), while others wrap it completely around the index finger (b) or pinkie (c). The key is to keep your index finger pointing up.

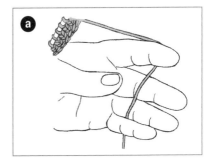

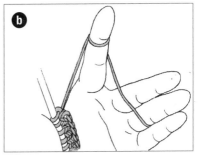

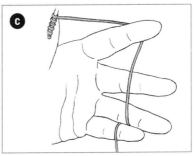

1. Holding the yarn in back of the needles, insert the tip of the right needle through the stitch on the tip of the left needle from left to right so the right needle pokes through to the back; the right needle should be underneath the left.

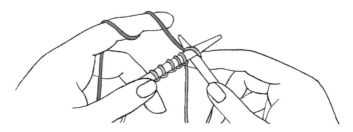

2. Using your left index finger to maintain tension on the yarn, reach the right needle tip behind the yarn and scoop it forward through the stitch (a). Let the old stitch fall off the left needle (b). Now do some more, and you are knitting!

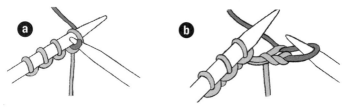

It's important to maintain some tension on the yarn to create even stitches. But be careful to avoid tightening the stitches while they are on the needle tips, as this will lead to stiff fabric and frustration on the next row when you try to poke your needle through those tiny, tight stitches. Instead, slide the stitch onto the body of the needle before gently snugging it.

PURL STITCH POWER

ENGLISH STYLE

1. Holding the yarn in front, insert the right needle tip into the stitch on the left needle from right to left, in the front of the stitch. The needle tips will be pointing in opposite directions and the right needle will be in front.

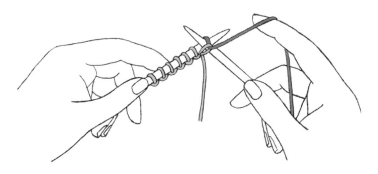

2. Wrap the yarn in a counter-clockwise direction, coming over the right needle tip, then under and back to the right.

3. Holding the wrapped yarn firmly, push the right tip out the back of the stitch (a), letting the old stitch fall off the left needle tip (b).

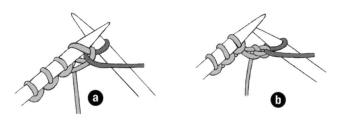

CONTINENTAL STYLE

The purl stitch can be a little trickier for Continental knitters, because you hold the yarn in front of the stitch. Experiment to find a hand position that works for you.

1. Holding the yarn in front, insert the right needle tip into the stitch on the left needle from right to left, in the front of the stitch. The needle tips should point in opposite directions, and the right needle should be in front.

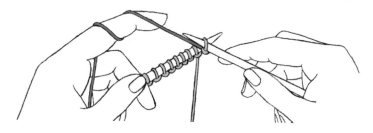

2. Bring the right tip under the yarn, out toward your body, then scoop over the top of the yarn (a) and pull it out through the back of the stitch (b).

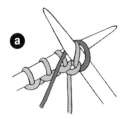

Pep Talk

Okay, now you're wobbling along with your training wheels. Some of you are feeling impatient to start barreling down the road, and others want to make sure someone is still running alongside, just in case. Wherever you are, that's great! Everyone learns at a different pace, both with our brains and with our hands. This is the point at which you have to let go of expectations and just keep going. Let it feel awkward and uncomfortable, and keep trying anyway. Step away from the judging and comparing, and just hang out with the process.

And that's just it: right now you are in the process stage. You will get to the product stage a little bit down the road, and then it will be about what you can make and who to give it to and when can you start knitting cashmere! I am here to tell you that you will get to the cashmere, and it will be worth it. For now, keep practicing your knits and purls, and look to the next chapters to start making curves!

SLIPPED STITCH SAVVY

YOU WILL SOMETIMES HAVE occasion to move stitches between needles without working them. This is called *slipping stitches*. It occurs during certain increases and decreases or special stitch patterns, and it's a very easy maneuver (as long as you distinguish your knits from your purls; see Reading Your Stitches on the facing page).

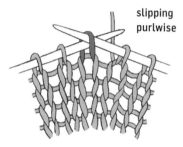

slipping purlwise

- **To slip a stitch purlwise,** insert the needle tip from right to left, as you would if purling, and slide the stitch to the other needle without working it. This is the default, if the pattern doesn't indicate otherwise.

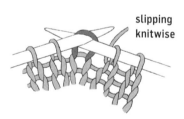

slipping knitwise

- **To slip a stitch knitwise,** insert the needle tip from left to right, as you would if knitting, and slide the stitch to the other needle without working it.

Remember: The default is to always slip the stitch purlwise unless the pattern specifies to slip knitwise.

READING YOUR STITCHES

KNOWING WHAT THE STITCHES LOOK LIKE is an important step in learning to knit independently, and it will empower you to find your place, fix mistakes, and more. Picture these words in flashing neon letters! That's how important they are.

Let's start with *stitch orientation*, which describes how the stitch sits on the needle. It's the same for both knit and purl stitches, and when you drop a stitch, it will be crucial information to have. (Notice I did not say "if," because you *will* drop stitches from time to time!) So, look at the stitches on your needle, and you will see that each stitch is a loop that straddles the needle. I think of it as the right and left legs of the stitch. The proper orientation of the stitch is with the left leg behind the needle and the right leg in front. Others think of it as the front leg being closer to the tip of the needle. However you view it, get it fixed in your mind, think of a clever way to memorize it (what works for me is to think of the phrase "out in left field," which tells me that the left leg should be away from me), and look closely whenever something feels off. If you were in my

STITCH ORIENTATION ON A NEEDLE

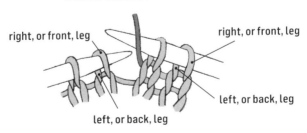

right, or front, leg

right, or front, leg

left, or back, leg

left, or back, leg

knitting class, I would go around and mess up your stitches and make you figure out how to get them all right again. This might be a fun game for you to play with a friend!

And just so you know, if the stitch is not oriented correctly on the needle, it will twist on the next row. Some knitters do this intentionally to achieve a specific effect, but for beginners, I recommend staying off the twisted path.

twisted stitches: front leg is behind back leg

Reading Edge Stitches

Because edge stitches are sometimes hard to read, they can cause a classic mistake that beginners often make. When you are starting a new row, the first stitch often wants to roll backward around the needle and ends up looking like two

first stitch rolling backward

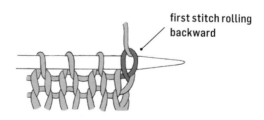

stitches instead of one, as in the illustration on the facing page. To avoid falling into this trap (and inadvertently increasing stitches), make sure to pull your yarn downward in front of the needle to straighten things out. Another tip to keep your stitch count steady is to recount your stitches every few rows.

Deciding Whether to Knit or Purl

When I start a new row, how do I know if I'm starting with a knit or a purl? You know by reading your pattern and by reading your stitches. Remember there are only two possible stitches, so we're in luck with this one. The knit stitch is the one people think of when they see a knitted garment. It is smooth and looks like a V hanging down from the needle (a). Purls, on the other hand, look bumpy and have a sideways strand of yarn wrapping the base of the stitch on the needle (b).

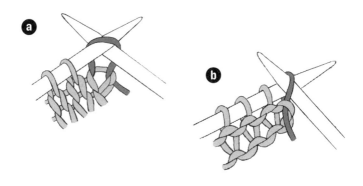

NAME THAT FABRIC!

Now that you've learned to knit and purl, it's time for some more language lessons. These two stitches can be combined in an infinite variety of ways to create a multitude of patterns. There are three big families that comprise the combinations of stitches that create the most common knitted fabrics.

Garter stitch produces a springy, ridged fabric. It is made by knitting every row or by purling every row. It looks the same either way. The key is that you do the same stitch every single row. Garter stitch is lovely, the rows are compressed, and the fabric is thick and will not curl up.

Stockinette stitch is what many people think of when they think of knitting. The right side is smooth, and you can see columns of V-shaped stitches. The wrong side is kind of bumpy and consists of interlocked U shapes. You create stockinette by knitting all the stitches on the right-side rows and purling all the stitches on the wrong-side rows. One fact that people forget to mention about this beautiful fabric is that stockinette will curl — that is, the bottom will roll up, and the sides will roll in; it's just pretty unruly. This makes it unsuitable for scarves (unless you want a tube), and it's why most sweaters have a band of ribbing or other stitch at the bottom to anchor the edge. If your knitted piece has the purl side facing out, it is called *reverse stockinette*.

Ribbing is what you get when you combine knits and purls within a row and repeat that pattern row after row, so the knits stack up above the knits and the purls stack up with purls.

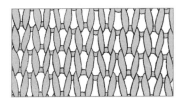

stockinette stitch

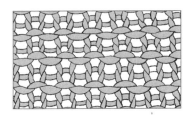

reverse stockinette

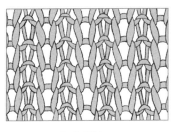

garter stitch

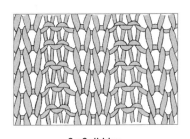

1 x 1 ribbing

2 x 2 ribbing

Ribbing lies flat — perfect for edges of stockinette fabric and scarf-like objects. Ribbing, by nature, will pull the stitches together, and yet it is stretchy, which makes it great for cuffs, necklines, and any place that needs some elasticity. Ribbing is very versatile: you can combine your columns of knits and purls in many ways. Single rib (knit 1, purl 1; sometimes called 1 × 1) and double rib (knit 2, purl 2; sometimes called 2 × 2) are most commonly used and give the greatest elasticity, but there are many variations to play with. The key bit with ribbing is that after the first row, you work the stitches as you see them. In other words, as you're working along on subsequent rows, knit the stitches that look like knit stitches and purl the purls. (Once again, refer to Reading Your Stitches, page 25, for advice on how to recognize each of these stitches.)

CHANGING TO A NEW BALL OF YARN

AT SOME POINT, YOU WILL NEED to add yarn to your knitting, whether it's a new ball because you ran out or because you want to spice it up with a little striping action. Either way, the technique is the same. I'll just start by saying that it is preferable to change yarns at the edge of your piece. It makes for a neater join and better opportunities for hiding the ends. If you are running low on yarn and aren't sure if you'll make it through the next row, just measure out what's remaining, and if you've got about three times the width of your piece, you're good to go for one more row. If not, start the new yarn now.

Begin by trimming the old yarn to about 6 inches, and hold that and the tail of your new yarn together. After working the first half-dozen stitches in the new yarn, you can let go of the tails and work to the end. At this point, you can tie the tails together in a square knot. Do not pull too tightly on this knot because you will take it out later when you weave in the ends. By securing the ends like this, you keep those edge stitches from being maddeningly loose. When you're done with the whole piece, go back and untie the knot, and weave the ends in (see page 34). Why not leave the knot? Because it's unsightly and uncomfortable. You don't want to spend all that time knitting a lovely soft scarf only to have a rough bump pressing into your delicate neck, do you?

BEGIN WORKING WITH NEW YARN

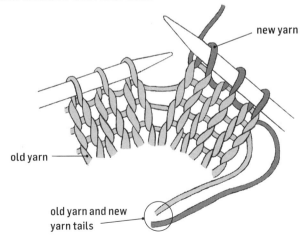

new yarn

old yarn

old yarn and new yarn tails

IT'S OVER: BINDING OFF

ONCE YOUR KNITTED PIECE is complete, you have to do something to secure all those loops in place. This is called *binding off* (some folks also call it *casting off*; the key word here is "off"). There are dozens of ways to bind off, some with very specific applications. For beginner purposes, I will show you the Traditional Bind Off. This is a very good technique that is useful for many situations and will stand you in good stead through most of your beginner projects. Once you begin to expand your skills and projects, I recommend learning other bind offs that can complement your work.

TRADITIONAL BIND OFF

This bind off can be done on either the knit or purl side of your work. I give instructions for knit stitches; if you are on the purl side, merely substitute purl for knit.

1. Knit the first 2 stitches.

2. From the front, insert the tip of the left needle into the first stitch you made (the one farthest from the needle tip) on the right-hand needle.

3. Pull it over the second stitch and off the needle.

4. Knit the next stitch and repeat the pull-over process (steps 2 and 3).

Continue this way across the row until you have one stitch left. Cut the yarn, leaving a 6-inch tail, and pull it through the loop and tighten. Voilà! You're done!

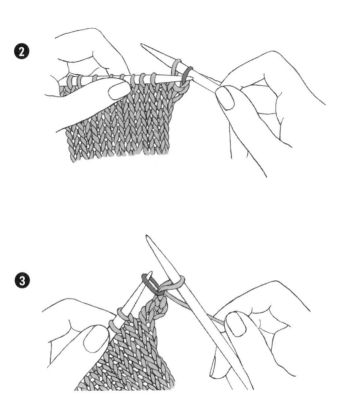

WEAVING IN THE ENDS

Now that you've bound off, there are still all those yarn ends hanging out, so you've got to hide them and make them stay put. Untie any knots where you joined yarn, and work with each tail individually. If you are going to sew pieces together, like for a sweater or a bag, you can leave the tails hanging until after seaming and then weave them in along the seams.

To weave in ends, thread the tail onto a tapestry needle (a short, blunt-tip needle with a large eye) and weave the yarn in and out of stitches on the wrong side of the fabric (through the purl bumps when working stockinette). When you have another tail at the same place, weave it a little above or below the first one to minimize the bulk.

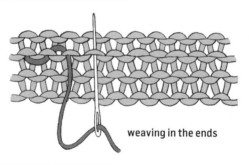

weaving in the ends

BLOCKING FOR THE PERFECT FINISH

Once you have finished the knitting, guess what — you're not done yet! The true finishing comes in the blocking process, which settles everything into its final position.

If you're knitting a garment, or anything with more than one piece, when is the best time to block? My preference is to block before seaming, for a few reasons. For one, you only have one layer of fabric to dry, which will be faster. It also allows you to make sure your pieces match up size-wise, and it sets the stitches, making seaming easier. Finally, blocking before seaming takes up less room than blocking the assembled garment and is less awkward to block. I can fit all the pieces of a sweater individually on my blocking board, but once it is sewn together, I have to use the bed or floor (not always convenient).

There are a number of ways to block, depending on fiber content and washing instructions for that particular yarn.

WORKING WITH MACHINE-WASHABLE YARN

Projects made with many cottons, some machine-washable wools, and most acrylics can be run through the washing machine on a gentle cycle. (To be sure this won't harm your fabric, always check the care instructions on the ball band before proceeding.) The ball band will also list the best procedure for drying, which usually involves one of the following:

- Run it through the dryer (on a cool cycle), if that's how you will be caring for it.
- Dry it flat, in which case, follow the instructions on the next page.

WORKING WITH ANIMAL FIBER (WET BLOCKING)

For most projects made with animal fiber, I prefer the immersion method, which is pretty much the same way you will wash it. Wet blocking, especially step 5 on the next page, allows you to convince the yarn to listen to you and adjust itself a bit. You can usually stretch things slightly, or squoosh those too-long sleeves a bit shorter. It's not going to miraculously rescue the gauge issue you refused to take seriously (see What the Heck Is Gauge?, page 56), but it does increase the fudge factor. And the beauty is that it relaxes and transforms the stitches, evening things out and giving your piece a professional, finished look.

1. Fill the sink with cool water and add some wool wash (your yarn store should carry a good-quality brand). Settle your piece into the wash and force it to duck under all the way. Be careful not to agitate and anger the felting deities, but you can do some gentle squishing. (See The Dreaded Felting, page 72.)

2. Leave it to fully saturate and soak for 15 minutes or so. Drain the water out and rinse if necessary, being careful to keep the water from running directly onto the fabric (again, to avoid felting). (Many of the newer types of wool wash don't require rinsing — yay!) While your piece is still in the sink, squeeze as much water out as you can, resisting the urge to twist and wring.

3. Have a big, thick towel ready and lift the piece onto it (please, oh please, do not let it hang dripping — and stretching — from your hands). Spread it out a bit on the towel, and then roll it all up. Squeeze the bundle, maybe even step on it a few times to extract more moisture.

4. Lay the piece flat somewhere, such as on a towel on the bed, on the floor, or on a table. Although it won't be dripping wet, you may want to put an extra towel underneath to keep your blocking surface from getting damp. Keep these things in mind when you choose the spot to lay out your piece:

   • It needs to stay flat the whole time it is drying.
   • It may take a while to dry (i.e., the thick sweater on the bed may be a bad idea).
   • If you need to shape it, you will be poking pins into the underlying surface.
   • It is preferable that the dog and/or cat does not nap on it.

5. Gently nudge the knitted piece into shape. Use a measuring tape to set the dimensions of your pattern, pinning the corners first and then working your way down the edges. With some things, you may not even need pins; other pieces, such as lace, require pins and a stern voice.

6. When the piece is dry, remove all pins and marvel at your creation!

BLOCKING WITH STEAM

Instead of soaking the knitted item, you can block with a steamer or an iron that has a steam setting.

1. Follow steps 4 and 5 on page 37 for pinning the dry piece.

2. Hold the iron or steamer a few inches above the fabric and let the steam saturate the fibers. Whatever you do, *do not* rest the iron on the item you are blocking. It will crush any textured areas and blur stitch definition.

3. When the piece is dry, unpin it and wear it with pride!

CHAPTER 3

SHAPING UP YOUR KNITTING:
INCREASES & DECREASES

Scarves and washcloths are popular projects for beginning knitters because they are just rectangles and squares. (For sample projects, see page 90.) Eventually, however, you may yearn for something more, and that will lead to the need for shaping. It's really a simple concept: to make it bigger or wider, you add stitches; to make it smaller or narrower, you subtract stitches.

When we move from concept to reality, however, suddenly things are different. Don't panic; there are many levels to which one can take knitting, and we, my friend, are staying with the stuff that falls under "all-purpose." This is what learning is about: start with the basics and add the finesse once you get comfortable. I'm giving you the information about finessing, but I encourage you to just learn these techniques at first, and then, once your hands are comfortable, engage your brain to notice the subtle differences that these various increases and decreases can make in your work.

EXPLORING INCREASES

SAY YOU NEED TO ADD some stitches to your row to make the row wider. There are a few ways to increase, and they all look just a bit different. The first two I am going to show you are fairly innocuous and work well for most situations. The third one, the yarnover (abbreviated as *yo*), leaves a little hole, like an eyelet, which is annoying unless you *want* a hole there. I'm including this option, however, because it is a very common maneuver and essential for any lace pattern.

Although increases can be executed on the purl side as well, most patterns have you do the shaping on the right-side rows, so I am providing just the knit versions here, except for the purl side yarnover (page 43).

KNIT INTO FRONT AND BACK (kfb)

Simple and easy to execute, this increase leaves a tiny bar across the increased stitch. Most of the time, that's not a big deal, but it will be more noticeable with thicker yarns. Here's how to work it:

1. Knit into the stitch as you would normally, but do not let the stitch fall off the left needle when done.

2. Instead, reach the right needle tip around to the back side of the left needle, insert the right needle tip through that same stitch, wrap the yarn around, and pull the stitch through.

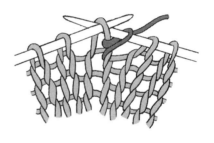

3. Now let the stitch fall from the left needle. You have made two stitches from one.

MAKE ONE (M1)

This increase is much less visible, making it my preferred increase for most situations. It can be done only between stitches, however, so it is unsuitable when the increase needs to be right on the edge, or when you are starting with only a few stitches.

1. Look closely into the gap between the needles, and locate the strand of yarn that runs from the base of the stitch on the left needle to the base of the stitch on the right needle. Put your left needle tip under this strand from back to front.

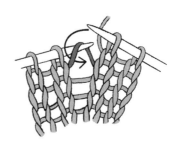

2. Insert your right needle into this strand, entering from the front and from left to right. This is as you normally knit, but it looks funny because that strand

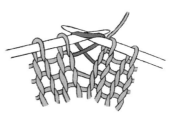

is twisted. This is good, because it prevents a hole from forming there. Wrap the yarn around and knit this new stitch, letting the strand fall off the needle. You just created a new stitch and you'll barely be able to see it.

YARNOVER (yo)

As an increase, the yarnover technique has its drawbacks, specifically the fact that it leaves an obvious hole. But sometimes you may want holes as a decorative element (think lace), and it's such a commonly used maneuver that I want you to know how to work it. It is done just as it sounds: the yarn is wrapped around the needle before working the next stitch.

- **Knit side.** Bring the working yarn between the needle tips to the front of the work. Wrap the yarn over the right needle tip to the back of the work, then knit the next stitch.

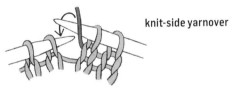

knit-side yarnover

- **Purl side.** The working yarn is already in front of the work, so wrap it over the top of the right needle tip and all the way back to the front. Then purl the next stitch.

purl-side yarnover

The yarn always wraps around the needle *counterclockwise*, whether you are working it between knit stitches or purl stitches (or even a combination of both). The key is to start with the yarn in front and wrap it over the top and around into position to work the next stitch. It will help if you use the tip of your right index finger to hold the yarnover in place while you work the next stitch. On the next row, just knit or purl into that strand of yarn when you come to it.

Finessing Your Increases (and Decreases)

Increases and decreases cause the affected stitches to lean to the left or right, leading to the designations of "left-leaning" and "right-leaning." Often this won't matter, but there are times when you may want to create a visual line (or mirrored lines) with your stitches. At this point, you can step up your game and learn which techniques produce which slants, and then use them in the appropriate places. Online resources, such as knittinghelp.com, and more in-depth technique books provide this information.

MASTERING DECREASES

Decreasing is a way to remove stitches, one or two at a time, across a row. Depending on where the decreases are placed, this will cause the fabric to either draw in or create an inward slope. (*Note:* If you need to remove more than two stitches in one spot, you should use a bind off instead of a decrease.) I am going to show you how to work some single decreases. I will point out which way the decrease leans, so that you'll be familiar with the technique whenever you're ready to go to that level. In the meantime, know that either of these techniques produces a lovely decrease.

KNIT 2 TOGETHER (k2tog)

This is a right-leaning decrease.

Insert the right needle tip through the front of the second stitch, then through the first stitch on the left needle from left to right. Wrap the yarn and pull the stitch through, letting the 2 old stitches fall off the left needle. And that's it!

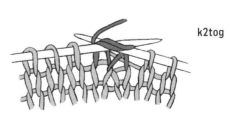

k2tog

SLIP, SLIP, KNIT (ssk)

This is a left-leaning decrease.

1. Insert the right
    needle into the first
    stitch on the left
    needle as if to knit,
    and slip the stitch to
    the right needle with-
    out knitting it (this is
    called *slipping knitwise;*
    see page 24).

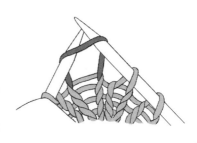

2. Do the same with the next stitch: you now have two
    unknit stitches on your right needle.

3. Slide your left needle
    into these two
    stitches from left to
    right, in front of the
    right needle. Wrap
    the yarn around the
    right needle and
    pull the new stitch
    through to the front,
    letting the 2 old
    stitches drop off the
    left needle.

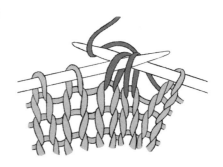

CHAPTER 4

WE ALL MAKE MISTAKES

You're looking at your knitting, and you see a mistake: This is the "deer in the headlights" moment. And it's not the mistake that is so scary; it's the "What do I do now?!" feeling that paralyzes us. Fear not! Learning to fix mistakes will empower you to move forward with confidence, because strength comes from the tools and knowledge of how to correct things, not from the impossible wish that nothing will ever go wrong. Believe me, we all rip back at some time; I did it just last week — two rows of 769 stitches each! Tedious, yes, but I did survive!

RESCUING DROPPED AND RUNAWAY STITCHES

DROPPED STITCHES ARE A common gaffe and one that is easier to deal with the sooner you notice it. What happens is that a stitch falls off the needle, and if you don't notice right then, it begins to undo itself, row by row (often called *running*). If you notice it soon after it happened, it's quite easy to fix.

PICKING UP A DROPPED STITCH

1. Working on the right side of the piece, slide your stitches between needles until the dropped stitch is positioned between the needle tips.

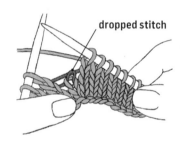

dropped stitch

2. With your right needle tip, pick up the dropped stitch, going into the loop from front to back.

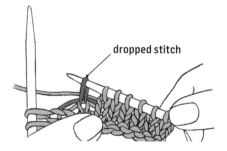

dropped stitch

3. Again, with your right needle tip, pick up the loose strand of yarn below the dropped stitch, also from front to back. Use your left needle tip to pull the loop of the dropped stitch over the loose strand and let the loop drop off.

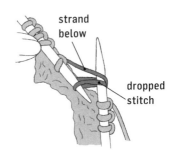

strand below

dropped stitch

4. Transfer the fixed stitch back to the left needle by putting the left needle tip into the stitch, again going from front to back (see step 2).

Dropped stitches can also be picked up on the purl side. The process is the same, just reverse the direction your needle enters the stitch and lifts the strand of yarn, going back to front in this case.

PICKING UP A DROPPED STITCH ON THE PURL SIDE

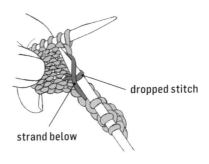

dropped stitch

strand below

FIXING RUNAWAY STITCHES

Runaway stitches are the ones that dropped and unraveled down several rows. The easiest thing here is to use a crochet hook that is one or two sizes smaller than your knitting needle to work the stitch back up, one row at a time. I prefer to work this fix on the knit side of the fabric. If I'm on a purl row when I discover the mistake, I just turn the work around to the right side to do the pickup and then turn back to the purl side when done and continue with my purling. If your fabric is garter stitch, you will need to alternate working from the front and back with each row.

1. Work across the row until the dropped stitch is between your needle tips. You will see the loop of the dropped stitch at the bottom of a ladder formed by the strands that unraveled.

2. Insert a crochet hook into the dropped stitch from the front. Grab the first loose strand of the ladder with the crochet hook and pull it through the stitch (a). Continue working up this way, pulling the ladder strands through one at a time to create a new loop (b), until you are back to the top.

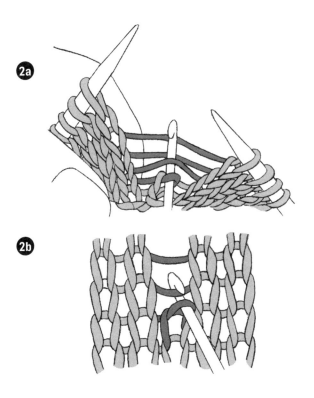

2a

2b

3. Transfer the stitch from the crochet hook to your left needle. The strands of the ladder may be tight to work with, especially if the stitch ran far. Sometimes, if the stitches were knit loosely, the section will even itself out, but other times the repaired stitches will look smaller. You will have to decide if that is so noticeable that you must proceed to the steps in the next section.

WHEN RIPPING BACK IS THE ONLY OPTION

RIPPING BACK IS A NECESSARY EVIL. Knitters try to sugarcoat it by giving it quaint nicknames, like having to "tink" (that's *knit* spelled backward) or "frogging" (can you say "rip it, rip it"?). But it all still comes down to having to un-do and then re-do. And while I do not live in the "every-stitch-must-be-perfectly-perfect" camp, I do know that some errors need to be fixed or they will haunt you forever and ruin the piece you are working so hard to create.

When confronted with this situation, you will have to decide if it is worth the time and headache to go back. Will anyone (but another knitter) ever notice? Will it be the first (and only) thing you see every time you wear or use it? Know your comfort level with this, and know that you will answer differently for different pieces. And don't forget, there are no knitting police. Let's start with the easy one: ripping back a partial row.

RIPPING OUT A SHORT DISTANCE

You just noticed a mistake back near the beginning of the row; now what? Well, you unknit back to that point.

1. Hold your needles as usual and poke the left tip into the stitch *under* the one on the tip of the right needle from front to back, and slide it over to the left needle.

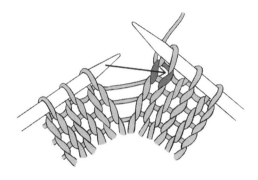

2. Tug the end of the yarn so it pulls out of the back of that stitch.

3. Keep doing this until you get to where you want to be. Then fix the glitch, and move forward again.

RIPPING OUT SEVERAL ROWS

Ripping back multiple rows is exponentially more scary than ripping out a short distance, but it does have the benefit of reinforcing everything you (should) know about how the stitches (should) sit on the needles. You could unknit one stitch at a time, but you'll probably want to poke your eyes out before you're done (three hours later); so take a deep breath and stay calm.

1. Find where the mistake is and mark that spot with a locking stitch marker or a bit of yarn.

2. Pull the needle out of the stitches (gasp!). Hold the piece in one hand and gently pull the yarn to unravel the stitches back to the row *above* the one you are aiming for.

3. Decide which hand is more comfortable holding the needle, and work from that side to the other. For instance, hold the empty knitting needle in your right hand and the knitted work in your left hand, and unravel one stitch at a time, working from the right edge to the left. Pick up each unknit stitch on the needle from back to front so that you are placing the stitch on the needle in the correct position. Work across the row until all stitches are back on the needle.

    To work from the left side, hold the needle in your left hand and the work in your right hand. Working from the left, you will be picking up the stitches from the front side.

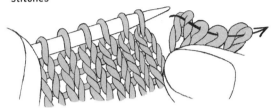

picking up unknit
stitches

Dealing with Kinky Yarn

Sometimes the raveled yarn is kinky and curly because it locked itself into the form of the stitches. This is especially the case if the piece sat for a while before you got up the nerve to deal with it. Cut the yarn, leaving a tail to weave in, and start with new yarn.

As for what you cut off, it's easy to refresh the kinked stuff. Wrap it around your hand and elbow to make a loop, and use some scraps of yarn to tie several places around the loop to keep all the strands under control. Soak your skein in cool water, squeeze out the water, and roll it in a towel. Then just hang it over a towel rack and let it dry. Roll it back into a ball, and it's ready to be knit.

WHAT THE HECK IS GAUGE?

WHEN YOU ARE FOLLOWING a pattern or knitting something to set measurements, gauge is the foundation to getting it right. *Gauge* refers to the number of stitches and rows per inch. You will see it written on the yarn ball band (see pages 75–76 for more details) as well as in the pattern (see page 79). If you want your piece to match the dimensions of the pattern, you *must* replicate that gauge exactly. This is not the place for fudging!

....

Consequences of Wrong Gauge

This is where I attempt to scare you into always and forever making a gauge swatch. Imagine you're going to knit a lovely sweater for Grandpa in his favorite shade of green. The finished sweater will be 40 inches around (his size exactly), and the pattern calls for a gauge of 4 stitches per inch. You knit your swatch and it measures 4.5 stitches to the inch. That's close enough (you think), and you spend several weeks knitting away. When you lovingly present the sweater to him for his birthday, he struggles to pull it over his head and . . . oh no! Your overachieving sister quickly does the math and points out that while the 160 stitches you cast on would have made a perfect 40-inch sweater at 4 stitches per inch, your gauge of 4.5 stitches per inch turned it into a 35.5-inch skintight disaster. And you just got your first lesson in how a "tiny" half-stitch difference makes all the difference in the world. The moral of the story: be precise! Accept no substitutes for proper gauge!

....

The Importance of the Swatch

How do you know if your knitting will match the gauge? This is where the swatch comes in. When starting a project, knit a small swatch of fabric using the yarn the pattern calls for and the needles you plan to use. (If the pattern yarn isn't available, and you need to make a substitution, see Data about the Yarn, page 79, for advice.) At a minimum, this swatch should be 4 × 4 inches. The purpose of the swatch is twofold.

First, it tells you if you can match the gauge of the pattern. If your gauge is spot on, congratulations, you are good to go! If it's off, even by a half stitch, you need to change needle size and knit some more. (See Consequences of Wrong Gauge, on the facing page, for why this is so important.)

Secondly, and this point is often overlooked, it shows you how the finished fabric will look and feel. Sometimes you can get gauge, but the resulting fabric doesn't look or feel the way you want it to, especially if you've made a yarn substitution. It may be too stiff or too drapey; it may be too loose and unable to hold up to the size of the pattern; it may not show the stitch pattern well. Take time to evaluate the swatch for both gauge and the look and feel of the fabric. Better to make changes now, *before* starting the project, than to end up with something unwearable after spending umpteen hours and precious money creating it.

Knitting a Swatch

Check the pattern requirements first. Does the pattern give the gauge in stockinette stitch or in the pattern stitch? Whatever the pattern designer used, you need to do the same thing. If the gauge is in stockinette, cast on at least 4 inches worth of stitches (for instance, four times the number of stitches recommended as the gauge for that yarn) plus 6 more stitches; then when you knit the swatch, you can knit the first and last 3 stitches on each row. This gives you a border of garter stitch (knitting every row), and your swatch will lie flat. For this same reason, I always start and end each swatch with 6 to 8 rows of garter stitch.

If the gauge measurements are in a pattern stitch, it will usually say "X number of stitches over 4 inches in pattern," and you can use that number to cast on. If it gives pattern gauge in stitches per 1 inch, multiply that number by 4. For both methods, I add extra stitches and rows to create a garter-stitch border. A flat swatch is much easier to measure than one that curls.

Measuring for Gauge

After you've worked your swatch, wash it as you plan to wash the finished piece, either in the washing machine or by hand. Do not pin or stretch it while drying; you want to see how it will behave naturally. Once it is completely dry, lay it flat on a hard surface. Take a measuring tape, ruler, or gauge-check and lay it on top of the swatch. Count the number of stitches in a 4-inch section and divide it by 4 to get the number of stitches per inch. Some gauge-checks have a 2-inch window, and it's fine to count the stitches in that and divide by 2; but measuring over a larger area will give a more accurate number. If the pattern calls for a gauge in a pattern stitch, it may be easier to count the number of stitches the pattern calls for in a 4-inch area and measure to see if you did indeed get 4 inches.

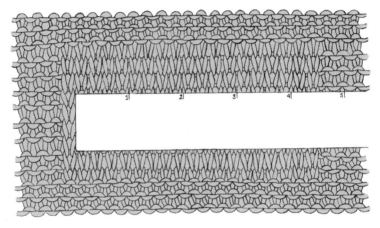

THIS SWATCH gets 16 stitches in 4 inches.

Adjusting Your Gauge

Gauge can usually be changed by switching the size of the needle you are knitting with. Because every person holds the needles and yarn differently, the needle size given in the pattern or on the yarn ball band is actually just a suggestion, a place to start. You will learn over time whether you tend to be a tight or loose knitter, or somewhere in between. If your swatch is off, try to adjust the needle size as follows:

- **If you have too many stitches per inch,** the knitting is too tight, and you need to use a larger size needle.

- **If you have too few stitches per inch,** your knitting is too loose, and you need to use a smaller size needle.

Sometimes changing the needle size is all it takes to get gauge. But sometimes that change causes you to end up with an unsuitable fabric. This is where you have to look at your swatch with a critical eye and ask if it will work for the item you want to knit. Is it firm enough for that jacket? Too stiff for the flowing shawl? Crisp enough to show the details in those beautiful cables? The swatch is your friend and will help you answer these questions so that your end result is what you want it to be.

Oh, and one more thing: check your gauge every once in a while as you are working on your project. Oftentimes, our hands relax when knitting for long periods, which can change the gauge (not to mention the effects of anger, stress, an extra glass of wine, and so on). Make sure you're staying on target with your gauge.

CHAPTER 5

GETTING DOWN TO THE TOOLS AND MATERIALS

Although knitting requires a very simple set of equipment and materials — two sticks and a string! — there is an overwhelming array of choices available today. And along with those choices are an equal number of often strong opinions about what is ideal. The best advice I can give you is to see what works for you. You will probably develop favorites, in both your tool and fiber choices. Keep an open mind, try out the new, and pay attention to how it feels in your hands. Develop your own opinions and expect them to change with skill levels and projects.

NEEDLES ARE NOT ALL ALIKE

NEEDLES ARE THE FUNDAMENTAL tool of the knitter. And because everybody is different and every project is different, there are many options for needles. A lot of it comes down to personal preference and what works best for your hands in a particular situation. When starting out, try different types and styles of knitting needles. And even continue these trials when you branch out into new knitting techniques and different kinds of yarn. The size number of the needle describes how thick it is. In general, the thicker the needle, the thicker the yarn that's appropriate to use with it, although there are exceptions. (For instance, lacework often uses needles much larger than the yarn size in order to create an open, lacy fabric.) Needle sizes are standardized, but (naturally, sigh) they are labeled differently according to US and metric systems. See the table in the appendix on page 102 for equivalents.

Choosing among Needle Types

Patterns often suggest what type of needle to use, but you may prefer to substitute another style that's more comfortable to you, if it works for the item you're knitting (see Circular needles, page 64). Also, though I love the economy of interchangeable sets, it's a good idea to hold off on investing in a set until you've knit projects with a few different types of needles.

Straight needles are also called *single points*. They have a tip on one end and a stopper on the other. Used for knitting flat pieces, they come in short (9- to 10-inch) and long (13- to 14-inch) lengths.

Double-pointed needles (DPNs) have points at both ends and come in sets of four or five needles. They are generally used for small pieces knit in the round, such as socks, mittens, and sleeves. They are available in a variety of lengths, most commonly 4 to 10 inches, though longer ones are available.

NEEDLE TYPES

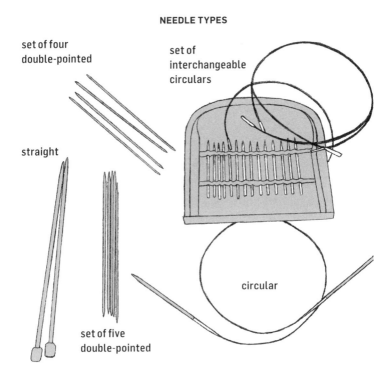

set of four
double-pointed

set of
interchangeable
circulars

straight

circular

set of five
double-pointed

Circular needles consist of two needle tips connected by a cord (usually nylon). They can be used to knit circular pieces in the round, or flat pieces back and forth. When knitting a circular piece (such as a hat), you will need a cord length that is less than the circumference of your piece. Circular needles are sold in a range of needle sizes, as well as in fairly standard lengths (9, 12, 16, 24, 32, 40, 47, and 60 inches); the length is measured from tip to tip and includes both needle ends and the cord.

Interchangeable circular sets, available in any of the various needle materials, have needle tips in an array of sizes accompanied by cords in a variety of lengths. The tips attach to the cords either by screwing or twisting. These sets are usually a very flexible and economical option, once you know which type of needles (wood, bamboo, metal, and so on) you prefer to work with.

New Kids on the Block: Square Needles

These needles have appeared within the last five years, and as the name says, they are square instead of round. They are available in both wood and metal, in all the various needle types. The theory is that they are easier on the hands because squares don't roll in your hands, thus you grip them less tightly. The corners may also have the advantage of creating a space, which makes it easier to slide the tip into the next stitch. Also, the tips tend to be pointier, always helpful for lace projects. What I know is that I love them, and I think it's worth giving them a try to see if they work for you.

Finding the Needle That's Right for You

You are soon likely to discover that you prefer different needle materials depending on the characteristics of your yarn. For instance, I use metal needles for many projects when I want to knit fast, wooden ones for socks when I don't want the stitches to slip off, and the sharpest tips I can find for lace knitting.

- **Aluminum** is lightweight, and stitches slide well; the needles are noisy and cool to the touch.
- **Nickel-plated** needles are slick, speedy, and cool to the touch.
- **Brass** is not as slick as nickel; it's great for lace and cool to the touch.
- **Bamboo** is lightweight and warm, less slippery, and less noisy than metal needles.
- **Wood** is warm, more slippery than bamboo, but less so than metal.
- **Plastic or acrylic** needles are lightweight and warm, and the least slippery of all materials.
- **Carbon fiber** is warm and strong, and gets smoother with use.

A Public Service Announcement from Your Author . . .

Differences in needle materials can produce differences in gauge. Therefore, be sure to knit your swatch with the same needle material that you will use for the whole project.

ACCESSORIES ADD TO THE FUN

THE KNITTING WORLD IS FILLED with fun and functional accessories. As you continue down the path, you will likely collect a range of tools specific to the techniques you choose. For beginners, here is a list of items to carry in your knitter's tool kit:

- Small scissors with sharp points and some kind of protector for the tips
- Tape measure
- Needle and swatch gauge. This has holes, to slide a needle into to check its size, and a ruler, to measure the gauge of your knitting.
- Stitch markers. These small rings slip onto your needles and mark important points in your knitting (for example, where to increase, decrease, begin the pattern, and so on). They can be plastic, rubber, or metal in a closed or open ring, or even ones that look like coiless safety pins.

Beginner's Tip
When you're first learning to knit, choose a pair of short (9- or 10-inch) single-point bamboo needles. They are easy to handle and are not too slippery, so the yarn will be more likely to stay on the needles. Choose a size appropriate for your yarn (see How to Read a Yarn Ball Band, page 75.

- Row counter to keep track of where you are
- Tapestry needles or large yarn-sewing needles for weaving in ends and seaming
- Crochet hook for picking up stitches. Size C is good for many rescue jobs.
- Emery board for smoothing dry fingertips and nails that snag the yarn
- Sticky notes or highlighter tape to mark on the page where you are in a pattern

SOME ESSENTIAL TOOLS

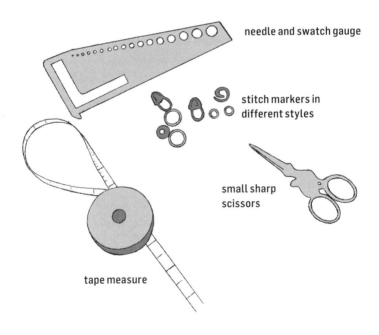

needle and swatch gauge

stitch markers in different styles

small sharp scissors

tape measure

- Knitting/project bags. These can be anything from a small bag or container to carry your accessories, to a large bag with pockets and compartments for your tools, pattern, and current project. I am continually amazed by the ingenuity and variety of ways knitters carry their gear — everything from handsewn drawstring bags to office-supply containers to voluminous shoulder bags. My own collection, ahem, is not to be trifled with.

THE REAL MAGNET OF THE KNITTING WORLD: YARN

As you will discover, yarn comes in an infinite variety of weights, fibers, and textures. It can be a bit mind-boggling and overwhelming at first; for now, just enjoy the feel and color. And speaking of feel, what about "scratchy" (imagine I am saying that in a pinched, whiny voice)? This is a very personal matter, and what irritates one person will be perfectly comfortable to another. A good test is to rub the yarn on the sensitive skin of your neck or cheek and see how it feels. Although some people really are allergic to wool (or to some wools), many people who are convinced they are allergic to wool have, in fact, just been subjected to coarse wool that was scratchy. There are many very soft wools, and superwash wools in particular can work well for the super-sensitive folks.

The Craft Yarn Council of America has a coding system to describe the weights of yarn; I've put that chart in the appendix (page 103). For now, here are some brief descriptions of the various weights. What you should know is that, while we use these terms to describe the weights, when you knit a pattern, the most important information is the gauge — how many stitches per inch.

Yarn Weights

Laceweight. This very fine, wispy yarn knits up at 8 to 9 stitches per inch, though generally you will see it knit on larger needles to achieve the ethereal light and open qualities of lace.

Fingering. Knit at 7 to 8 stitches per inch, this is the weight used most commonly for socks.

Sport. This knits at 6 stitches to the inch and creates thin, lightweight garments.

DK. This knits at 5½ stitches to the inch and is often used for baby knits and lightweight garments. DK stands for *double knitting*, a term that originated in Great Britain and referred to a yarn weight between worsted and sport. There is also a technique called double knitting, but that does not relate to the weight of yarn; don't let it confuse you.

Worsted. This is sort of the workhorse, middle-of-the-road gauge that many, many sweaters are knit with. It knits at 4 to 5 stitches to the inch, which is a pretty big range, so always check the specific gauge of your pattern.

Aran weight. This type of worsted yarn knits at 4 stitches to the inch.

Bulky or chunky. This yarn knits up at 3 to 3½ stitches per inch and create thick, dense fabric. But, oh, does it knit up fast!

Super bulky. This includes anything thicker than 3 stitches to the inch. There's not much drape, but it's super thick and warm, and very quick to knit.

COMPARATIVE YARN WEIGHTS

lace

sport

worsted

bulky

A World of Yarns to Try

The yarn family is a diverse and growing one, with new fibers and blends being added regularly. There are four main categories: animal, plant, man-made, and cellulosic (a hybrid of plant fibers and man-made processing). Within these groups is a staggering number of options and a wide variety of characteristics. There are some generalizations; for example, animal fibers are warm and elastic, plant fibers are cool and nonelastic, natural fibers are breathable, and man-made fibers are easy to care for. As with all things knitting, there are exceptions to these groupings and there are personal preferences. And to add to the mix, many companies are now creating beautiful yarns by blending fibers to enhance their strengths and minimize challenges. For example, adding wool to plant fibers increases a yarn's elasticity and memory; Tencel spun with wool adds a sheen and makes the fabric that is knit with it more fluid and drapey.

ANIMAL FIBERS

Wool comes from sheep, which would make you think it's all alike. But no, it's not. Fleece characteristics vary from breed to breed; some are coarser, some softer, some stronger, and so on. Wool has memory and will usually hold its shape well, but it will felt if subjected to agitation and warm water. Wools labeled "superwash" have been treated to prevent shrinkage and felting when machine-washed; some, but not all, of these yarns can be machine-dried, so always read the ball band's care instructions and test a swatch first. Wool is warm and stays warm when wet, making it ideal for outerwear in winter.

Alpaca comes from, well, alpacas. The fiber is very soft and even warmer than wool, warm enough that you may want it blended with another fiber to avoid sweating in a large garment. Adding other fibers also gives the alpaca some stability, as its density and lack of crimp makes it prone to stretching (and not bouncing back). Llamas are cousins to alpacas, and the yarn from their fiber shares the same characteristics.

Mohair is from goats — they're called angora goats, confusingly enough (see also Angora, below). Fuzzy and fluffy, this yarn can add loft to a project. The fibers are so long, you can knit mohair on large needles and the fuzz fills in the space, creating airy, delicate pieces.

Cashmere is the irresistibly soft, downy undercoat from cashmere goats. Incredibly fine and luxurious, though usually expensive, it is warm and lustrous.

Angora comes from rabbits. It is as soft as a cloud and oh-so-tempting. However, it is best used in moderation as it is also quite warm, tends to shed, and will felt incredibly quickly. It's probably best in a blend or as an accent.

The Dreaded Felting

When a fiber felts, it shrinks and mats together. (You know, like that favorite sweater that accidentally went through the laundry and now fits your Chihuahua?) Many animal fibers, especially wool and mohair, felt or mat easily if subjected to temperature changes and agitation.

Silk is produced by silkworms and is strong, lustrous, shiny, and soft. It produces fabric that drapes and flows and has a beautiful sheen. If your garment calls for shaping and elasticity, look for silk blended with wool.

The rest of the gang. Fiber is harvested from numerous other animals, but they are not big players on the scene because of the means of obtaining their fiber or other challenges. These include qiviut (downy undercoat of the musk ox) and possum, bison, mink, and camel fiber.

PLANT FIBERS

Cotton is cool and absorbent, strong, and comfortable to wear. Cotton doesn't have the elasticity of wool, so it may stretch out and not bounce back, though washing will often restore the original shape. The other thing to watch with cottons is the weight: it is heavier than animal fibers, and in big pieces, such as afghans or large sweaters, the weight may be too much to hold the shape.

Linen comes from the flax plant and is extremely strong. Like cotton, it lacks elasticity, but its strength makes it great for bags, and it can be knit into crisp, cool tops. Linen softens immensely with each washing.

Hemp is made from the hemp plant and behaves similarly to linen.

THE RAYON FAMILY: CELLULOSIC FIBERS

These fibers were born of the desire to create an artificial silk. Rayon is a hybrid of natural plant fibers and a man-made process. The plant is pulverized, soaked in various solutions, and then extruded into fibrous threads, which are spun into yarn. Most of the yarns in this group share the same characteristics; the variations are mostly dependent on which plant they were derived from. They tend to be smooth and silky with a bit of a sheen. They are not very elastic and can stretch out, though blending with wool will improve their ability to maintain shape. *Viscose* is a word often associated with these fibers; it refers to the specific process of creating the yarn.

The list of fibers produced this way includes rayon (from wood pulp), modal (from beech trees), lyocell (also known by the brand name Tencel, from wood pulp), bamboo, soy, corn, sugarcane, seaweed, and milk protein. I'm sure the list will continue to grow.

....

Beginner's Tip

Choose a worsted-weight yarn in a solid, light color (easier to see stitches) for learning to knit. Something that is a single ply (one strand) or a tightly twisted plied yarn will make it easier to avoid splitting the yarn. Skip the fuzzy, furry, multicolor, or thick-and-thin yarns.

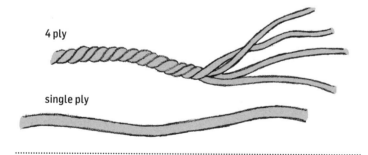

4 ply

single ply

....

SYNTHETIC FIBERS

Synthetic fibers are created through chemical processes. Although some knitters can be snobbish about using only natural fibers, synthetic yarns do possess qualities that are desirable in knitting. For starters, they are very easy to care for — usually machine washable (except in novelty blends) — and they are generally inexpensive. And for those who are allergic to wool or who live in warm climates, synthetics are the answer. That said, you should know that a synthetic yarn will not keep you warm like wool, nor will it breathe well, and so it may also overheat you in warm weather.

Synthetic yarns include nylon (often added to sock yarns due to its great durability), polyester, and acrylic. Sometimes you will find a yarn that lists microfiber, which is just an extremely fine synthetic fiber.

How to Read a Yarn Ball Band

The band of paper that wraps your ball, skein, or hank of yarn contains a wealth of information that can help you understand how to use it. Companies vary in how much information they put on the band, but the basics should be there. Always, always keep a ball band from each batch of yarn (you'll thank me for it later!), with a sample of the yarn attached to it. I work in a yarn store and spend hours each day helping people who can't remember what yarn they were knitting, trying to track down the color, and guessing at dye lots.

Here's the information you should find on the ball band:
- Company name and yarn name
- Fiber content, usually listed in percentages
- Weight of skein, either in grams or ounces, sometimes both (50 grams = 1.75 ounces)
- Number of yards in the skein. If it tells you the amount just in meters, add 10 percent to calculate the yards. For example, 90 meters = (about) 100 yards.
- Color number or name
- Dye lot number. This is very important. All the yarn that goes into the dye pot together should match. If you use yarn from different dye lots, you may end up with a distinct line where the color changes from one dye lot to another. Often you will not notice the color difference in the skein, but it can be horribly noticeable when knit. Always buy enough in one dye lot to finish your project.
- Suggested gauge and needle size
- Care instructions (hand wash, machine wash, iron or not, and so on)

CHAPTER 6

LEARNING TO DECIPHER PATTERNS

As with most things written, there is no standardized template for knitting patterns. Especially with the explosion in the number of independent designers, the Internet, and self-published patterns, the industry has few constraints on how patterns are written.

Fortunately, we can count on a certain amount of commonality in how the information is presented. I'll assume you like the photo of the finished object (which, by the way, is called an FO in knitting parlance) and are now trying to figure out if you can make it. The first bit you want to look at will usually be near the top of the pattern; it's the lowdown on the basic parameters of the pattern — size, type of yarn, gauge, and so on. Let's dissect these bits, shall we?

SIZES AND MEASUREMENTS

LOOK CLOSELY AT THIS, because there are two sets of measurements that may be presented, and you want to know which you are looking at. It may say "fits chest size 34" (38", 42")"; that refers to the size of your body. Additionally (or instead), it may say "finished size 36" (40", 44")"; this is what the sweater will measure at the chest when you are done knitting it. If you are not sure what size you need, measure a sweater that fits the way you like, compare those measurements to the pattern's, and pick the finished pattern size closest to that.

One more thing about the size: notice how the second and following sizes are all contained within parentheses? This will be mirrored throughout the basic info section and the entire written pattern instructions. The pattern lists everything with the numbers for the first size, followed by the numbers for the other sizes in parentheses, in exactly the same order each time. So if you are knitting the 44" size in a pattern with sizes 36" (40", 44", 48"), and it says you will need 10 (12, 14, 16) skeins of yarn, then you, personally, will need 14 skeins because 44" and 14 skeins are both the second numbers in the parentheses.

Non-sweater-type patterns usually come with just the finished dimensions. Child and baby garments are often described by age, though they may list finished size as well. These age designations are generally all over the map, so if you measure an actual child near that age, you have a better chance at a successful fit.

DATA ABOUT THE YARN

THE PATTERN USUALLY INDICATES the manufacturer and brand name of the yarn used in the photography, and, ideally, the fiber content and yardage for that yarn. It also tells you how many skeins are required. Of course, you don't have to use the same yarn that the original designer used, but this information gives you the total yarn yardage you will need. If you substitute another yarn, it is more accurate to go by the number of yards needed rather than weight, as different fibers and spinning processes create yarns with more or less yardage for the same weight as the original. Additionally, and most importantly, a substitute yarn must match the gauge called for in the pattern. Which brings us back to gauge.

The Bottom Line Is Gauge

The pattern gives the gauge you need to match if you want your FO to look like that beautiful picture. The gauge is often measured over 4 inches, in which case you will divide the number of stitches by 4 (for example, 20 stitches over 4 inches = 5 stitches per inch). The other thing to watch out for is whether the gauge is for stockinette or pattern stitch. If it is in stockinette, you can knit your gauge swatch in the normal manner (the assumption is that if your stockinette gauge is spot on, your pattern stitch will be as well). However, if it says, for instance, "gauge is 29 stitches over 4 inches in Bluebonnet Lace stitch," then you must knit your swatch in Bluebonnet Lace stitch.

The bottom line here is that *your gauge must match*. No ifs, ands, or buts. Do not fool yourself into believing otherwise. You probably remember that I harped on this in chapter 4, but it's so critical that I am nagging you again here!

Needle Size: Just a Suggestion

Okay, now I've got to nag you about this, too. Because when a pattern gives a needle size, it is just a suggestion. Yes, just a suggestion, and it's based on some average knitter or designer somewhere who got gauge with that particular needle. But we are all different: some of us are tight knitters, some are loose, and some are in the middle. So you try the yarn with that needle and see what happens; if you don't get gauge, then you should adjust your needle size and try again (see Adjusting Your Gauge, page 60). Eventually, you will know where you fall on the spectrum and automatically adjust even before the first swatch. (My sister drops down two needle sizes every time!) The point I'm trying to make is that the most important thing is matching gauge, not matching needle size.

Another thing to note is what type of needles they want you to use: straights, double points, or circulars. And see if there's anything else needed. This could be anything from knitting aids such as stitch markers, stitch holders, and tapestry needles, to other materials such as buttons, beads, and so on.

TRANSLATING KNITTING SHORTHAND

IT STARTS WITH THE ABBREVIATIONS, the clumps of unintelligible letters and numbers that appear to mean something if only you could speak the language. Fear not!

If your pattern is in a magazine or book, there's probably a table of abbreviations in an appendix, with specialized stitches explained on the pages of the patterns where they appear. On individual patterns, the abbreviations are usually listed either at the beginning or the end. In the appendix (page 103), I've compiled a list of common abbreviations. You do not need to memorize this list, but you'll find that you'll learn most of the frequently used abbreviations pretty quickly. The others you can look up as needed.

The other thing to understand is how all those abbreviations are strung together so that you know what to knit (or purl, as the case may be). Fortunately, this is pretty standardized. Each row has a set of instructions. I like to think of it as reading a sheet of music: the symbols show you where to repeat certain parts and what every stitch ("note") should do.

The asterisk (*) shows you what to repeat.

Example: **Row 1:** K2, *K3, P3; repeat from * four times, K2.

Translation: Knit 2, then repeat what is between the asterisks for the given number of times (in this case knit 3, purl 3 four times), and end with knit 2.

Parentheses can be used in two ways, so look closely. They are used most commonly to separate stitch counts for individual sizes.

Example: **Row 1:** Cast on 80 (88, 96, 104) stitches.

Translation: Cast on 80 stitches for the smallest size, 88 stitches for the next size, and so on. This will occur throughout the pattern whenever the stitch count varies for different sizes. If you highlight numbers for your size, it will be easy to stay on track.

Parentheses are also used to designate repeats, and in those cases, you will see the end parenthesis followed by the number of times to repeat.

Example: **Row 1:** K3, (yo, K1) five times, K2.

Translation: This means you will knit 3, then repeat a yarn-over and knit 1 five times, and end with knit 2.

Sometimes you get a row with parentheses for both repeats and size designations.

Example: **Row 42:** K3, (yo, P1) 3 (4, 5) times, K3.

Translation: Knit 3 and then yarn over and purl 1 three times for the first size, four times for the next size, and so on; end all sizes with knit 3.

Brackets may also be used when things get more complex. I won't overwhelm you with that now; it's starting to feel more like an algebra lesson. For the moment, I think we can just stick with the sheet music analogy.

WORKING WITH PATTERN STITCHES

OFTEN A PATTERN INCLUDES a certain repeating stitch pattern (sometimes more than one!), written out before the main instructions and then referred back to within the pattern instructions. For instance, it might say something like this:

BLUEBONNET LACE STITCH

Row 1. K1,* yo, k2tog; repeat from *; end K1.

Row 2. Purl all stitches.

Row 3. K2,* yo, k2tog; repeat from *; end K2.

Row 4. Purl all stitches.

Repeat Rows 1–4 for pattern.

And then when you get to the part of the knitting where you are to use the stitch pattern, you'll find something like this: "On next right-side row, begin Bluebonnet Lace and work this pattern stitch until the piece is 14" long." You then refer back to the pattern stitch directions and continue knitting on your merry way.

LEARNING TO READ KNITTING CHARTS

FOR PATTERNS WITH MORE COMPLICATED stitch patterns and colorwork, the pattern may include charts. These look like graph paper with hieroglyphics. Of course, the pattern will include a key to the hieroglyphics! People (like me) who see things in patterns and shapes often find charts easier to work from than written-out instructions. Others are more comfortable with text. One is not better than the other; the best choice is what works for you. Check the pattern you're thinking of using to see if it uses charts, words, or both, and decide which you prefer to rely on, depending on what works best for you.

Oh, Dear . . . Pattern Errata

It's not a dirty little secret anymore but an acknowledged reality that patterns get published with mistakes. Don't even worry about how this happens, just be proactive. Before you begin a pattern, check online for pattern corrections, or *errata*, as they are known. You should be able to find them on the website of whoever was responsible for publishing the pattern, including the publisher (book or magazine), yarn company, or individual designer's website or blog. You can also look the pattern up on Ravelry.com and see if others who knit it encountered problems. In the excitement of beginning a new project, it's hard to remember to do this. But this will be your clue to whether something is wrong with the pattern: no matter how many times you knit and reknit this one section, it's still not coming out right. Do not assume that you are inept. Check for errata. (And then if you still can't figure it out, find someone to help you.)

STAYING ON TRACK

KNITTING IS ONE OF THOSE ACTIVITIES where you rarely finish what you start all in one sitting. We usually knit for a while and then put it down because, well, life happens; we come back to it sooner or later. Another challenge is the frequent interruptions that occur in the midst of knitting, all of which means that you need tools and strategies for keeping track of where you are and what comes next. So here are a few tips.

Stitch Markers Are Your Friends!

I have these in little containers all over the house and use them to remind me of my place. I start with them at the beginning: I place a marker every 10 stitches as I cast on to make it easier to count where I am. There's nothing like the frustration of counting 148, 149, 150, . . . "Mom, where's my backpack?"! It's much quicker to count (and recount) by tens. I also use these lovelies to mark my stitch repeats. If I make a mistake, I then catch it at the next marker, instead of at the end of the row. You can even use different-color markers to stand for different things, for example, green for the beginning of a circular round, pink for the stitch repeats, and blue for decrease points. And if I'm knitting a piece where it's difficult to tell right side from wrong side (like in garter stitch), I clip one of those markers that looks like a coilless safety pin to the right side so I don't get confused.

Keeping Track of the Pattern

Tracking your place in the pattern can be done in a few ways. If you're following a stitch pattern, you can use a row counter to show where you are. A few varieties of these are available; some look like the clickers they use to count people at sporting events, some fit over your needles and you twist to move the numbers, and of course, "there's an app (or 300 apps) for that." The main thing to remember is to establish a consistent pattern for when you change the number. I always click to the next number at the end of the row. That way I know what's next when I come back to knit some more. Again, consistency is what is important here.

You can also use paper and pencil to keep track, of course: check off the rows or make little hatch marks. If you're working off a photocopy of your pattern, you don't have to worry about being confused by those marks when you make the pattern again because you can just make a new copy from the original.

And, finally, on the pattern instructions, you can use a variety of things to underline the row you are currently working on, both to make it easier to see and to mark your place when you put your knitting on hold:

- **Sticky notes.** The most low-tech is the handy sticky note. Just place it on the page under the line you are reading and move it as you go.
- **Highlighter tape.** Then there's the fun and colorful highlighter tape. Lay it along or underneath the pattern line you are working; remember, consistent placement keeps you from guessing! This stuff peels off easily, and you just move

it along. Great invention and it lasts forever; I'm still working off the first roll I bought.

- **Magnetic pattern holder.** You can also get a magnetic pattern holder. This is a thin metal board that you place your pattern on. Magnets hold the pattern in place, and you position a long thin magnet underneath the row you're working. One advantage of this setup is that it usually has some kind of an easel backing so it sits upright on a table, which makes it easier to see.

....

Tracking Tips

When you start to knit a project, make a photocopy of the pattern and keep that with your knitting. Use a highlighter to mark all numbers that apply to your size; for example, if it says cast on 58 (63, 67, 71) stitches, highlight the number you need for your size. Also take notes about any modifications you make. Then if you decide to knit it again in a different size, you can start fresh with a new copy from the original, plus you can refer to your notes from the first go-round. Please note that making copies for your own use is acceptable in this case, because you already purchased the pattern. Copying patterns to share with others cheats the designer out of the profits for his/her creativity and hard work (as well as being a violation of copyright laws).

....

- **Apps.** You can always go high-tech and find an app for your electronic device of choice. The capabilities of these vary, but you can find many that track multiple inputs at once (row count, pattern repeats, decrease points, and so on).

....

Is This Pattern Too Hard for Me?

This is a very personal question, because the answer depends not only on the competence but also on the confidence of the knitter. I've seen people knit incredibly complex and difficult things early in their knitting life just because no one told them the project was too hard for them, and they really wanted to make it. And I've seen folks who have been knitting for 30 years who still won't knit a sweater.

This is the guidance I offer you: Look at the pattern. Do you really want to make them? Skim through the instructions: Do you understand the basics of them? Do they scare you? If you're not totally comfortable with the instructions, do you have a friend or local yarn store (LYS to knitters) that can help you through the tricky bits? And if the instructions feel intimidating, what skills do you need to learn before you tackle the project? Cables? Working on double-pointed needles? What it really comes down to is the strength of your desire to make this particular thing, coupled with the confidence that you can do it. I believe that you can knit anything, and I also know that sometimes you need to learn a few more techniques to do it successfully. No one can tell you if the pattern is too hard except you, based on a realistic assessment of the pattern.

....

MULTIPLES AND TOTAL STITCH COUNTS

EACH OF THE STITCH PATTERNS in the projects that follow gives you a "multiple-plus" number, such as "multiple of 4 + 3 stitches." This means that when you are estimating how many stitches you should cast on for the width of the scarf you have in mind, using the pattern stitch given, you must do a little math. For example, if the pattern stitch is a multiple of 4, begin your calculations by multiplying the width in inches you want, times the stitches per inch recommended *on the yarn ball band*. Add to that the additional number of stitches required to fill out the pattern stitch. If the resulting number is not a multiple of 4, round up or down to get the correct number.

For example, for a 7-inch scarf and a stitch gauge of 4½ stitches per inch, multiply 7 × 4½ for a total of 31½ stitches. Your chosen pattern calls for a multiple of 4 + 3 stitches. The nearest multiples of 4 are either 28 or 32. Add the extra 3 stitches to those numbers and you get 31 or 35 total stitches. With 31 stitches and a gauge of 4½ stitches per inch, your scarf will measure 6.9 inches wide. With 35 stitches, your scarf will be 7¾ inches wide. You can then decide which size you want and cast on the appropriate number of stitches. Because size is generally not critical in a scarf, you have some leeway in playing with those numbers.

After casting on the desired number of stitches, follow the instructions on the following pages for the scarf (or scarves) you want to knit.

A SET OF SIMPLE "RECIPES" FOR SCARVES

HERE ARE SOME BASIC stitch patterns you can use to make beautiful scarves that will lie flat. They're a great way to practice your knits and purls and to sneak in a little pattern reading, too. Most of these will look similar on both sides, so hang a stitch marker on the row 1 side to help keep track of where you are.

Finished Measurements
Approximately 7" × 60"

Yarn
These scarves can be knit with any yarn/gauge. Choose your yarn and buy the yardage amount below based on your choice.
- DK or sport weight: 600 yards
- Worsted weight: 300–350 yards
- Bulky weight: 250 yards

Needles
Straight needles, 10" long, in the size listed on the yarn ball band

A Freeform Knit Scarf
Just make it up as you go! Mix rows of ribbing with rows of garter, throw in stripes of color – just play around and have fun. Remember that stockinette stitch will curl, so mix knits and purls within the rows or do stretches of garter stitch to keep things flat.

A WIDE RIB SCARF

(Multiple of 6 + 3 stitches)

Row 1. K3, *p3, K3; repeat from * to end of row.

Row 2. P3, *k3, P3; repeat from * to end of row.

Repeat these 2 rows until you run out of yarn or until the scarf is as long as you want. (You really don't want to run completely out of yarn: make sure you have a length of yarn left that is four times as wide as your scarf for the bind off. Note that when you work this pattern correctly, you will be knitting into knit stitches and purling into purl stitches on both sides.)

Bind off. Weave in the ends. Block the scarf according to fiber type (see Blocking for the Perfect Finish, page 34).

WIDE RIB SCARF

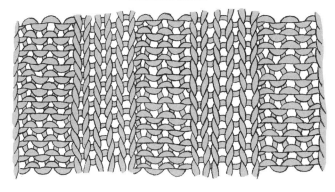

A MISTAKE RIB SCARF

(Multiple of 4 + 3 stitches)

This looks like it should be a standard 2×2 (or K2, P2) rib, but because of the last P1, it is offset by one stitch and makes a beautiful corrugated fabric.

Row 1. *K2, P2; repeat from * to last 3 stitches, K2, P1.

Repeat Row 1 until you have a length of yarn left that is four times as wide as your scarf.

Bind off. Weave in the ends. Block the scarf according to fiber type (see Blocking for the Perfect Finish, page 34).

MISTAKE
RIB
SCARF

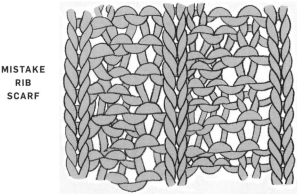

A WAFFLE STITCH SCARF

(Multiple of 4 stitches)

Row 1. Knit.

Row 2. Purl.

Rows 3 and 4. *K2, P2; repeat from * to end.

Repeat Rows 1–4 until the scarf is nearly as long as you want it, then repeat Rows 1 and 2 once more. To make sure you don't run out of yarn, you should leave a length of yarn at least four times the width of your scarf.

Bind off. Weave in the ends. Block the scarf according to fiber type (see Blocking for the Perfect Finish, page 34).

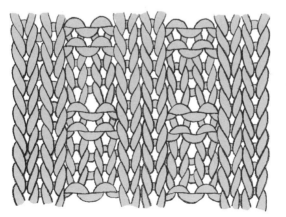

WAFFLE STITCH SCARF

A BASKET-WEAVE SCARF

(Multiple of 8 stitches)

This is a fun one to play with because you can vary the size of the blocks however you want: make them squat and wide, tall and narrow, even asymmetrical. You can also throw in rows of knits between the blocks (between rows 5 and 6, or rows 10 and 1). Have fun with it!

Rows 1–5. *K4, P4; repeat from * to end of row.

Rows 6–10. *P4, K4; repeat from * to end of row.

Repeat Rows 1–10 until scarf is desired length. Make sure you leave a length of yarn that is four times as wide as your scarf for the bind off.

Bind off. Weave in the ends. Block the scarf according to fiber type (see Blocking for the Perfect Finish, page 34).

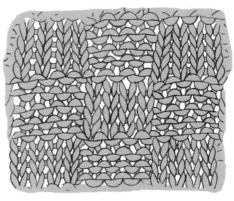

BASKET-WEAVE SCARF

RECIPE FOR A KNITTED WASHCLOTH

Don't laugh! A handknit washcloth is a fine thing — soft and cozy (or knit it with a rough yarn for exfoliating), the perfect size (because you decide what that will be), and a great hostess or baby shower gift. Plus, it is an excellent opportunity to practice your increases and decreases.

MATERIALS

- A cotton or cotton-blend yarn and the needles in the size called for on the yarn ball band; a 50-gram ball should be sufficient.

INCREASE ROWS

To begin, cast on 3 stitches.

Row 1. Kfb, K1, kfb. (Remember kfb? That's an increase where you knit into the front and back of a stitch. See page 41 for a refresher.)

Row 2. Knit all stitches.

Row 3. K1, inc 1, knit to last stitch, inc 1, K1. (After the first row, you can choose which increase method to use.)

Row 4. Knit all stitches.

(continued on next page)

Repeat rows 3 and 4 until the washcloth is desired width. The knitted piece will resemble a triangle at this point: Measure one of the sides from the needle to the tip to determine width. (The length across the needle is the diagonal of the cloth.)

DECREASE ROWS

As with the increases, you can choose whichever decrease you want to practice.

Row 1. K1, dec 1, knit to last 3 stitches, dec 1, K1.

Row 2. Knit all stitches.

Repeat these 2 rows until you have 5 stitches remaining.

Next row. K2tog, K1, k2tog.

Next row. Knit all stitches.

Last row. K2tog, K1, pull decrease stitch over last stitch, cut yarn, and pull through last stitch. Tighten to finish.

You can leave a tail long enough to make (or even crochet) a loop for hanging the washcloth. I recommend washing and drying the washcloth a few times before using to soften it up.

NEXT STEPS

WHAT TO DO NOW that you're ready for more? Frankly, from here on you are the driver, and your passion, enthusiasm, and confidence will lead you. That said, I encourage you to practice your stitches to increase your proficiency and consistency. I compare this to the hours I spent practicing scales and finger exercises at the piano, wondering why I had to do that when all I really wanted was to play Beethoven. Once I could play Beethoven, I was grateful for the practice, because it strengthened my hands and built the command and agility I needed. And that is the reason for practicing your knitting as well.

The good news is that practicing your knitting can actually produce something more exciting than trills and chord progressions. In the appendix, I've included yardage information for a variety of simple projects so you can make beautiful things while working on your skills. I like squares and rectangles because they make the perfect palette for stitch combinations, without the added complications of shaping. Plus, they are a little more lenient in case of gauge discrepancies.

You can peruse the stitch dictionaries, such as those by Vogue Knitting and Barbara Walker, — listed in the appendix (page 104), to find stitch patterns you like and then work them up in one of your projects. Because the yardage guidelines on pages 100–102 are listed according to gauge, you can pick whatever yarn you like, use the recommended size needle for that yarn, and create something beautiful.

THREE THINGS THAT MAKE A GOOD KNITTER

THAT'S IT. I've got you started, and I wish you well. I leave you with these thoughts:

1. **Mastering the physical moves of knitting.** When learning to knit, one thing that helps is to adopt a child-like attitude and persevere in the face of frustration. Yes, it will feel awkward at first, and you will probably produce some "interesting" fabric. Don't give up! Over time, the process will smooth out and feel more natural. Your hands will become familiar with the motions, and you will find the hand positions that work for you. Be patient and recognize you must put in the time to become fluid and comfortable with your knitting. All those friends who tell you that knitting is relaxing and enjoyable are right; don't despair if you don't feel it immediately. You're learning something new, after all. Cut yourself some slack and let yourself be a beginner.

   Developing the physical skills of knitting will take some time, but it will pay off. As your hands (and your mind) relax, you'll venture into new territory and learn new techniques. And your skills will grow. What once seemed daunting becomes the next thing to try. Mastering the mechanics of knitting allows you to take on greater challenges.

2. **Learning to "read" your knitting.** This does not refer to reading a pattern, but rather to actually seeing what is

going on in your knitting. This understanding frees you to catch mistakes and fix them, and it makes you less dependent on a person, book, or video to tell you what's going on. So learn to see how stitches should sit on the needle. Learn to recognize the difference between how knit and purl stitches look. This knowledge empowers you to find your place within a stitch pattern without endless counting. It enables you to become a thinking knitter, and gives you the freedom to create what you want. It allows you to finesse your knitting and take it to a deeper level.

3. **A desire to learn.** You're already on your way — you've picked up this book! Honestly, one of the big differences between good knitters and those who just knit things is having curiosity and desire. I've learned that there's no such thing as "too hard" if the person really wants to make it. Good knitters stretch themselves, learn new techniques, fall in love with a project, and knit it even though someone told them it wasn't appropriate for a beginner. They learn how to finesse their knitting by using stitches that enhance the look or function of their project. In turn, this learning develops confidence as knitters build the skills to create.

I know, lofty thoughts, while all you really want is to pick up the needles and yarn and get at it! These are just some principles to keep in mind as you cast on your knitting foundation.

APPENDIX

Yardage Guidelines for Items You Might Like to Knit

Scarves

It's hard to identify a "standard" size for a scarf, as bodies and preferences vary. The yardages listed in this chart are for a 60" scarf, which is usually good for one wrap around the neck. These are just approximate amounts: Add an extra 5% if you want fringe. If your pattern has a lot of texture stitches, add another 15 to 20%.

GAUGE (STS/IN)	6" WIDE	8" WIDE
3	150 yds	225 yds
4	250 yds	325 yds
5	300 yds	425 yds
6	425 yds	575 yds

Baby Blankets

Knitting for babies is so satisfying, because the projects are quick to complete and so completely unique. For the sake of the parents, please use a machine-washable yarn. And don't skip over the wool — the superwash wools these days are very soft and snuggly; they will provide warmth and breathe well.

GAUGE (STS/IN)	24" X 30"	30" X 30"	36" X 36"
3	325 yds	400 yds	575 yds
4	460 yds	580 yds	825 yds
5	620 yds	775 yds	1100 yds
6	875 yds	1100 yds	1575 yds

Shawls

Shawls ask for a little more thought in the planning. How far down the back or arms do you want it to come? For the width, you can measure from the nape of the neck, over the shoulder to just below the elbow, or you can measure from your neck down your back to the desired size.

The length will depend on the height of the person you are knitting for and how much you want it to wrap around. Will it just cross in the center front and be fastened with a shawl pin? Or do you want to wrap it around the front and then over the shoulder like a big hug? This chart lists a shorter/narrower option and the giant hug option. For other sizes, you can use these amounts to estimate what you'll need.

GAUGE (STS/IN)	18" X 60"	22" X 72"
3	475 yds	680 yds
4	700 yds	1000 yds
5	925 yds	1320 yds
6	1300 yds	1870 yds

Cowls

Cowls are a lovely addition to our wardrobes, a great way to whip out a quick project, and perfect for people like me who can't seem to make a scarf stay put without choking myself. And they are really simple, to boot! Basically, a cowl is a scarf with the ends stitched together. If you want something long, use yardages from the scarf chart above. For an Infinity Scarf, all you do is twist one end before seaming it together. For a loose, once-around-the-neck piece, use the chart on the next page to determine yarn amounts.

Cowls *(continued)*

GAUGE (STS/IN)	10" X 32"	14" X 32"
3	150 yds	200 yds
4	225 yds	275 yds
5	275 yds	375 yds
6	400 yds	525 yds

Knitting Needle Sizes

DIAMETER (MM)	US SIZE NUM	SUGGESTED YARN WEIGHTS
2	0	Superfine (sock, fingering, baby)
2.25	1	
2.75	2	
3.25	3	Superfine to fine (sock, fingering, baby, sport)
3.5	4	Fine (baby, sport)
3.75	5	Fine and light (baby, sport, DK, light worsted)
4	6	Light and medium (DK, light worsted, worsted)
4.5	7	
5	8	
5.5	9	Medium and bulky (worsted, heavy worsted, chunky)
6	10	Bulky (chunky)
6.5	10½	
8	11	Super bulky and multiple strands or unspun roving
9	13	

Standard Yarn Weight System

	0 LACE	1 SUPER FINE	2 FINE	3 LIGHT	4 MEDIUM	5 BULKY	6 SUPER BULKY
TYPE OF YARNS IN CATEGORY	FINGERING; 10-COUNT CROCHET THREAD	SOCK, FINGERING, BABY	SPORT, BABY	DK, LIGHT WORSTED	WORSTED, AFGHAN, ARAN	CHUNKY, CRAFT, RUG	BULKY, ROVING
KNIT GAUGE* (Ranges in stockinette; Stitch to 4")	33–40**	27–32 sts	23–26 sts	21–24 sts	16–20 sts	12–15 sts	6–11 sts
RECOMMENDED NEEDLE SIZE RANGE (Metric)	1.5–2.25	2.25–3.25	3.25–3.75	3.75–5.5	4.5–5.5	5.5–8	8 and larger
RECOMMENDED NEEDLE SIZE RANGE (US)	000–1	1–3	3–5	5–7	7–9	9–11	11 and larger

*   Guidelines only: The above reflect the most commonly used gauges and needle sizes for specific yarn categories.

** Laceweight yarns are usually knitted on larger needles to create lacy, openwork patterns. Accordingly, a gauge range is difficult to determine. Always follow the gauge stated in your pattern.

Common Knitting Abbreviations

Abbrev.	Description	Abbrev.	Description
BO	bind off	P	purl
CO	cast on	pm	place marker
dec	decrease	RS	right side
dpn	double-pointed needle(s)	sl	slip
inc	increase	ssk	slip, slip, knit these 2
K	knit		stitches together
kfb	knit into front and back of one stitch (increase)	st(s)	stitch(es)
		tbl	through back loop
K2tog	knit 2 stitches together (decrease)	WS	wrong side
M1	make one stitch (increase)	yo	yarnover

READING LIST

Bestor, Leslie Ann. *Cast On, Bind Off* (Storey Publishing, 2012)

Briar, J.C. *Charts Made Simple* (Glass Iris Publications, 2011)

Herzog, Amy. *Knit to Flatter.* (Stewart, Tabori and Chang, 2013)

Parkes, Clara. *The Knitter's Book of Yarn* (Potter Craft, 2007)

Radcliffe, Margaret. *The Knitting Answer Book* (Storey Publishing, 2005)

Vogue Knitting. *Stitchionary Volume 1: Knit and Purl* (Sixth & Spring Books; Reprint edition, 2012)

Walker, Barbara. *A Second Treasury of Knitting Patterns* (Schoolhouse Press, 1998)
—— *A Treasury of Knitting Patterns* (Schoolhouse Press, 1998)

ONLINE RESOURCES

Craft Yarn Council
www.yarnstandards.com
The Craft Yarn Council represents yarn companies, accessory manufacturers, magazines, book publishers, and consultants in the yarn industry, and sponsors a wide range of promotional and educational programs.

KnittingHelp.com
www.knittinghelp.com
Video tutorials of knitting stitches and techniques

Ravelry
www.ravelry.com
A combination of database, social networking site, and online personal journal for knitters and crocheters, Ravelry provides a wealth of information and connections for fiber folk. Use it to look up yarns; find patterns and designers; catalog and chronicle your own yarn, needles, and projects; and chat with other knitters in forums.

**WEBS America's Yarn Store
    YouTube Channel**
www.youtube.com/user/websyarnstore/videos
Video tutorials of knitting stitches and techniques

ACKNOWLEDGMENTS

The creation of a book like this, which involves much more than just writing, is the work of many people, and I am grateful for all the folks who have been a part of the birth of *How to Knit*.

Thanks to my publisher, Storey, for creating the Basics series and asking me to author the knitting book. I am a great believer in simplicity and loved the idea of a beginner's book that provides the important information without overwhelming the student. Thank you to the crew at Storey for not only encouraging and supporting my efforts, but also for adding their own expertise to the project: Pam Art, Kathy Brock, Ilona Sherrett, Cindy McFarland, and Theresa Wiscovitch. I am especially grateful for my wonderful (and wonderfully patient) editor, Gwen Steege, who once again put her confidence in me and helped keep my voice heard throughout the editing process.

I am also extremely fortunate to be able to work in the "industry": my day job is in a yarn store, and I am lucky enough to be surrounded by creative and talented people every day. Thank you to my colleagues at WEBS for your inspiration, feedback, and sense of humor. Even though I often groaned when you asked, "How's the book going?" it helped to know my moonlighting was supported.

I have learned much from my students over the years. Sometimes you taught me new techniques and ways of doing things, but mostly you taught me how to teach. You showed me how important perspective is and how two people sitting side by side do not necessarily see the same thing. You challenged me to find patience and compassion and new ways to explain things. You helped me see that just because something is easy for me doesn't make it easy for everyone. So I thank you for being my teachers, and I hope that this book reflects what I have learned from you.

And everything always comes back to the basics for me — my family. I am grateful for parents who taught me to love and appreciate learning, to strive for excellence and expertise. They also stood behind my decisions to follow my bliss, as wacky as it seemed at the time. I miss my mom, but I feel her influence in my creativity and strength and the person I have become. And I am thankful to still have my dad so close to continue to inspire me with his creativity and drive, and to turn to for advice and deep conversation.

Thank you to my photographer, my daughter Cady, for taking pictures of my hands for the illustrator to work from. I am so happy to have you be a part of this book. And I am grateful for the daily inspiration I get from you. You show me determination and perseverance and continue to be my greatest teacher. Best of all, you fill my life with laughter. Thank you!

INDEX

Italics indicates an illustration; **bold** indicates a table or chart.